CELEBRATING THE CITY OF JAKARTA

Celebrating the City of Jakarta

Walter the Educator

Silent King Books

SILENT KING BOOKS

SKB

Copyright © 2024 by Walter the Educator

All rights reserved. No part of this book may be reproduced in any manner whatsoever without written permission except in the case of brief quotations embodied in critical articles and reviews.

First Printing, 2024

Disclaimer
This book is a literary work; the story is not about specific persons, locations, situations, and/or circumstances unless mentioned in a historical context. Any resemblance to real persons, locations, situations, and/or circumstances is coincidental. This book is for entertainment and informational purposes only. The author and publisher offer this information without warranties expressed or implied. No matter the grounds, neither the author nor the publisher will be accountable for any losses, injuries, or other damages caused by the reader's use of this book. The use of this book acknowledges an understanding and acceptance of this disclaimer.

Celebrating the City of Jakarta is a little collectible souvenir book that belongs to the Celebrating Cities Book Series by Walter the Educator. Collect them all and more books at WaltertheEducator.com

USE THE EXTRA SPACE TO TAKE NOTES AND DOCUMENT YOUR MEMORIES

JAKARTA

A city rises, a marvel on verdant hills.

Celebrating the City of
Jakarta

Jakarta, your heartbeat hums a timeless tune,

A symphony of life from morning until noon.

Your skyline dances with the first light's kiss,

Steel and glass structures form an urban bliss.

Skyscrapers reach, fingers to the sky,

As if aspiring to whisper secrets to clouds passing by.

Oh Jakarta, with streets that never sleep,

Where cultures blend, histories deep.

Celebrating the City of
Jakarta

In markets bustling, life's colors bloom,

Aromatic spices, and sweet flowers' perfume.

Beneath the canopy of sprawling trees,

Lies the ancient wisdom carried by the breeze.

Temples and mosques stand side by side,

In harmony, a testament to tolerance's pride.

Your rivers wind like veins of old,

Whispering tales that remain untold.

From the harbor, where ships come and go,

To the alleys where children's laughter flows.

Celebrating the City of
Jakarta

Kota Tua, a remnant of days gone past,

Echoes of the Dutch, their shadows cast.

Cobblestones narrate stories of old,

In every corner, new memories unfold.

Night descends, a veil of indigo hue,

The city sparkles with lights anew.

From skyscraper to shanty, a unified glow,

Jakarta's spirit, a vibrant show.

Monas stands tall, a symbol in the night,

Its flame of independence burning bright.

A beacon of freedom, resilience, and might,

Guiding the city through darkness to light.

In the bustling hum of Menteng's streets,

Where modernity and tradition meet,

Coffee shops filled with artists and dreams,

Ideas flow like Jakarta's streams.

Ancol's shores with waves that play,

Where families gather to end the day.

Under the moon's gentle sway,

Laughter and joy, like tides, array.

Oh Jakarta, in your embrace,

One finds a home, a sacred space.

Through every moment, every place,

Your spirit, Jakarta, we forever chase.

Celebrating the City of
Jakarta

ABOUT THE CREATOR

Walter the Educator is one of the pseudonyms for Walter Anderson. Formally educated in Chemistry, Business, and Education, he is an educator, an author, a diverse entrepreneur, and he is the son of a disabled war veteran. "Walter the Educator" shares his time between educating and creating. He holds interests and owns several creative projects that entertain, enlighten, enhance, and educate, hoping to inspire and motivate you. Follow, find new works, and stay up to date with Walter the Educator™ at WaltertheEducator.com.

www.ingramcontent.com/pod-product-compliance
Lightning Source LLC
LaVergne TN
LVHW012049070526
838201LV00082B/3876